COLONIAL PEOPLE

The Shipbuilder

ANN HEINRICHS

Cavendish
Square

New York

Published in 2014 by Cavendish Square Publishing, LLC
303 Park Avenue South, Suite 1247, New York, NY 10010

CPSIA Compliance Information: Batch #WS13CSQ

All websites were available and accurate when this book was sent to press.

Library of Congress Cataloging-in-Publication Data

Heinrichs, Ann.
The Shipbuilder / Ann Heinrichs.
p. cm. — (Colonial people)
Includes bibliographical references and index.
Summary: "Explores the life of a colonial shipbuilder and his importance to the community, as well as everyday life responsibilities, and social practices during that time"—Provided by publisher.
Audience: Grades 4-6.
ISBN 978-0-7614-0005-9 (hardcover) — ISBN 978-1-62712-048-7 (paperback) — ISBN 978-1-60870-987-8 (ebook)
1. Shipbuilding—United States—History—Juvenile literature. 2. Shipwrights—United States—Juvenile literature.
3. United States—History—Colonial period, ca. 1600-1775—Juvenile literature. I. Title.
VM23.H36 2013
623.820973'0903—dc23
2011028344

Editor: Peter Mavrikis
Art Director: Anahid Hamparian
Series Designer: Kay Petronio

Photo research by Marybeth Kavanagh

Cover photo by MPI/Getty Images

The photographs in this book are used by permission and through the courtesy of: *The Image Works*: TopFoto, 4; LANKS/ClassicStock, 11; Mark Cator/Impact/HIP, 23; Kike Calvo, 25; Mary Evans/Pharcide, 42; *North Wind Picture Archives*: 8, 13, 37; *SuperStock*: 41; IndexStock, 17, 21, 39; Erin Paul Donovan, 34; age fotostock, 44; *The Colonial Williamsburg Foundation*: 26; *Landov*: Molly Riley/Reuters, 31; *Alamy*: Stockfolio, 32

Printed in the United States of America

CONTENTS

ONE

Shipbuilding in a New Homeland

Then let the sounds of measured stroke
And grating saw begin;
The broad-axe to the gnarled oak,
The mallet to the pin!

*—From "The Ship-builders,"
by John Greenleaf Whittier*

This poem celebrates the sawing, chopping, and hammering of shipbuilders at work. In the days of wooden sailing ships, these sounds echoed through every **shipyard**. Shipbuilding was a team project. It took many kinds of craftspeople working together to build a ship. Each one swelled with pride when the finished product set sail out upon the sea.

*A ship's carpenter pounds
in wooden pegs.*

New Colonies with New Needs

Shipbuilding was a booming industry in England in the 1600s. With its fleet of warships, England had one of the most powerful navies in the world. England was also expanding its country into a worldwide empire. English trading ships sailed to faraway lands in the Americas, the Caribbean, Africa, Asia, and the Pacific Islands. These ships brought back natural resources, farm products, and other valuable trade goods to England. As part of this trade effort, England also sent people to establish colonies in other lands. The **colonists** would settle these lands, govern the local people, and ensure a steady stream of trade goods.

English ships carried thousands of settlers across the Atlantic Ocean. These people set up colonies along the coast of North America. Some colonists hoped for more farmland than they could get in England. Religious groups such as the Pilgrims and Puritans made the journey so they could be free to practice their religion. Other colonists were **merchants** who hoped to expand their trading business.

Jamestown, in the Virginia colony, was established in 1607. It was the first permanent English settlement in North America. Ships began transporting tobacco from Virginia's Chesapeake region back to England in 1617. More shiploads of colonists crossed the Atlantic and made new homes along the coast, forming thirteen colonies.

Life was not easy in this strange new land. To build up a society from scratch, the struggling colonists needed craftspeople of all kinds. Fortunately, the new settlers included carpenters, shoemakers, bakers, barbers, and tailors. There were wheelwrights to make wagon wheels, coopers to make wooden barrels, and blacksmiths to make iron tools. All of these people served the needs of their communities. They also served the economic needs of the British Empire. The most valuable **cargoes** were sugar, rice, tobacco, and shipbuilding supplies.

Early colonists settled along the seacoasts, bays, and riverbanks. They especially needed boat builders and shipbuilders. Because roads were so bad, water travel was often the best way to get around. Ships were also needed for fishing and coastal trading. Whaling was an important industry for the empire. Whales provided oil that was used to fuel lamps and oil machines, meat to eat, ivory and teeth for decorations, and bone for various products. Whalers sailed out of Boston, Massachusetts, and traveled around the globe, sometimes not returning for up to three years. The cod fishing industry was important, too. It stretched from Cape Cod, Massachusetts, north past the French colony of Nova Scotia. Although many people could build small fishing boats themselves, they needed larger vessels to fish farther out at sea.

The Beginnings of Colonial Shipbuilding

Shipbuilders, also known as **shipwrights**, were among the first settlers in the colonies. They had learned their trade in the shipyards

Shipbuilders at Narragansett Bay, Rhode Island, 1613–1614.

of England. In 1607, a group of colonists settled at the mouth of the Kennebec River near today's city of Bath, Maine. However, they stayed for only a year. The winter had been dreadfully harsh, and relations with the area's American Indians were troubled. To get back to England, the colony's shipwrights built a fine ship that they named the *Virginia*. This was the first ship built by Englishmen in the American colonies. The sturdy *Virginia* made at least two Atlantic crossings.

In 1631, shipbuilders in Massachusetts launched the *Blessing of the Bay*. It was the first **colonial** ship built for trading purposes. Still, most of the early colonists' ships had been built in England. That began to change in 1640, when England plunged into a civil war. This distracted the nation's attention and energy from industries such as shipbuilding. At last, the American colonists had a chance to develop their own shipbuilding trade. By 1700, shipbuilding was a thriving colonial industry.

Colonial Shipyards

Soon shipwrights were opening shipyards all along the coast, from Maine in the north to Georgia in the south. Ships could be built more cheaply in the colonies than in England. Both land and labor were cheaper, and there seemed to be an endless supply of **timber**.

As a result, many English merchants began to have their ships built in the colonies. The English government even ordered many of its warships from colonial shipbuilders. By 1774, one-third of Britain's merchant ships were being built in the American colonies.

Shipwrights had a good eye for spotting ideal locations for shipyards. They chose places by the water where tall, hardwood forests grew nearby. A ready supply of forest trees was a must for building wooden ships. The seashore was a fine location. If possible, the shipyard was located along a sheltered **cove**, where waters were calm and the shore was protected from storms. Dozens of shipyards grew up along the many rivers that flowed into the Atlantic. Here, a finished ship could easily be sailed downstream to launch at sea.

On the other hand, large coastal seaport cities were good locations for shipyards, too. Merchants who wanted ships for transatlantic trading gave a lot of business to the shipyards. The merchants' dimly lit warehouses, stacked with barrels, sacks, and crates, stretched all along the harbor. Craftspeople of many kinds lived in seaports, too, and ships sailed in with needed shipbuilding supplies.

Massachusetts became the colonies' biggest shipbuilding center. Boston, Salem, Charlestown, and Scituate were bustling

Authentic replica of the **Susan Constant,** *which brought the first English settlers to Jamestown.*

seaport cities with lively shipbuilding industries. Early maps show that Boston had fifteen shipyards in 1722. The dense forests of New Hampshire and Maine provided acres of timber for shipbuilding. Thus Portsmouth, New Hampshire, and

Kittery, Maine, became known for their fine ships. Newport, Rhode Island; New York City; and Philadelphia, Pennsylvania, were shipbuilding cities, too. Philadelphia lay alongside the Delaware River, more than 50 miles inland and sheltered from the ocean storms, so many shipyards were clustered there. William Penn founded Philadelphia in the 1680s. By 1750, it was the largest city in the colonies and the center of trade and the shipping industry. Farther south were the shipyards of Baltimore, Maryland; Jamestown and Norfolk, Virginia; Charleston, South Carolina; and Savannah, Georgia.

Ships for Different Uses

Colonial shipwrights built two basic types of ship. One was a large vessel fit for voyages across the Atlantic Ocean. These huge, three-masted ships could hold a great deal of cargo. For transatlantic voyages, this was the ship of choice. Its sails were not attached directly to the mast. Instead, they were connected to **spars**, or wooden poles, set at a right angle to the length of the ship. Because the sails hung "on the square," this kind of ship was said to be square-rigged. The largest sails on a square-rigged ship were shaped like a trapezoid—a rectangle whose upper edge is shorter than its lower edge.

Colonial shipbuilders also made smaller vessels suitable for trading along the coast or fishing offshore. These vessels usually had fore-and-aft sails. That is, the sails hung in line with the ship's length, rather than at a right angle. Usually the sails were triangular, with a wooden spar called the boom at the bottom of the mainsail. With fore-and-aft sails, it was easier for the crew to shift the sails and catch the wind. Thus a captain

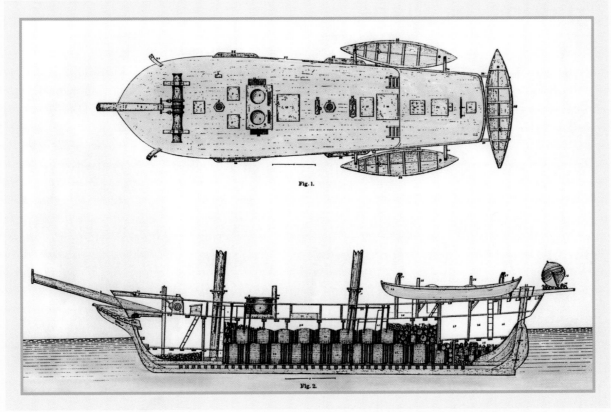

Plans for the whaling schooner Amelia *of New Bedford, Massachusetts.*

could easily navigate the jagged coastline. The most popular styles among these smaller ships were sloops and schooners. Sloops had one mast and two sails, one in front of the mast and one behind it. The larger schooners had at least two masts.

It could take as long as a year to build a large, seagoing ship. On the other hand, a shipyard could turn out a sloop or schooner in half that time.

Making the Plans

Shipbuilders could not afford to build ships in advance. Instead, they waited to receive an order from a customer and draw up a contract. This ensured that the shipbuilder would get paid. A contract called for the customer to pay part of the money right away. Portions were paid as the work went on, with the final payment made upon completion.

A shipbuilder's typical customer was a merchant. He told the shipbuilder what style of ship he wanted and how large it should be. This determined the price. Knowing the ship's size, the shipbuilder could tell how many workers he needed to hire for the job and what supplies he needed.

Ships' sizes were given in terms of **tonnage**. For example, a large merchant ship built to cross the ocean might be a 300-ton vessel. A smaller ship for coastal trade might be as small as 20 tons. However, tonnage has nothing to do with how much a ship weighs. Instead, it tells how much cargo a ship can carry. In colonial times, this measurement was not entirely exact. A colonial shipbuilder may have used one of England's methods to calculate tonnage. However, after years in the trade, he relied more on his own experience than on exact measurements.

After receiving a contract, the master shipbuilder designed the ship. He could imagine exactly what the ship would look like, though he may not have drawn up detailed plans. He may have sketched out a design on paper, using a compass to draw arcs, or sections of a circle, to outline the curved shape of the ship's sides. A carpenter made patterns out of thin wood and used them to outline the shape on shipbuilding wood. Then the pieces were sawed and taken to the building site.

Shipbuilding was the most complex of all the colonial crafts. A ship was built of wood, then fitted with iron parts. Sails were hung, sometimes dozens of them in many sizes. Rope was strung through sails and wood beams to control the sails and keep the ship on course. There was also navigation gear such as the compass. A completed ship was truly a work of art and the pride of many workers.

TWO

A Day in the Shipyard

Rising before dawn, the master shipbuilder takes just a few minutes' walk to reach his workplace. Along the way, he proudly surveys his holdings. Land in the colonies could be cheap, or even free. Some early colonial governors granted huge parcels of free land to settlers. In Virginia in the 1600s, for example, each man who paid his own passage to the colony was granted 40 acres of land. This shipbuilder owns his own shipyard, with room for building two or three ships at once. On the same plot of land are his home, a vegetable garden, a pasture, and acres of forestland.

It is summer in the shipbuilder's New England town, and the morning breeze carries the familiar smells of sawdust and the sea. The shipbuilder is pleased that the weather is warm and dry. Rain and cold temperatures affect the wood and keep his shipbuilders from working. With extra hours of sunlight, the

Replicas of colonial sailing ships in an Atlantic coast harbor.

workdays are long, too. For outdoor work like shipbuilding, craftspeople work from the first light of day until sundown. Here, that means the workday starts at 4:30 A.M.

The Shipyard Crew

As the owner approaches his shipyard, he sees his workers arriving. No one is a year-round employee, because shipbuilding cannot take place during New England's harsh winter months. Instead, the owner hires people on a temporary basis. At many points in the process, there is work for unskilled laborers to move materials from place to place or to work under the supervision of skilled craftsmen. He hires these men on occasion as "day laborers." The poor people in many cities rely on this occasional work. His most important worker is the foreman, who directs the crew's day-to-day activities. In the town's smaller shipyards, the master shipwright also acts as the foreman.

Among the shipbuilding crew are many skilled craftspeople. Some are well-established workers who have practiced their trades for years. The owner pays them for each day's work or for completing a specific job. Some crewmembers work as **indentured servants**. That is, they offer their labor in exchange for their passage from Europe to the colonies. As many as half the immigrants to the colonies arrived as indentured servants, some voluntarily and some against their will.

Some workers are black slaves whom the master shipwright owns. Other African Americans are indentured servants, and others are free men. Many slaves had been kidnapped in Africa and shipped to the colonies. Slave traders brought others from Caribbean islands such as Jamaica and Barbados. Slaves were not paid, they served until death, and their status passed on to their children. On the other hand, those who had been set free could earn wages for their work, and their children were born free.

Finally, every large shipyard used **apprentices**. These were boys who were learning the shipbuilding trade. Their parents or guardians had signed an apprenticeship contract with the master shipwright. According to this agreement, the shipwright would train the boy in the skills of the shipbuilding trade. The master fed and clothed the boy and gave him a basic education. One Virginia apprentice was guaranteed "to read the Bible and write in a legible hand." Often, the education consisted of learning reading, penmanship, and arithmetic well enough to keep records for a shipbuilder or a merchant. The boy should be able to list cargo items, supplies, and people's names, as well as to add up weights, costs, and wages.

A Step-by-Step Process

As the workday begins, sawyers are gathering around the sawpit. There they will saw the timbers and **planks** for the carpenters to use. The owner has a good supply of wood stacked nearby. Some timbers have been stripped of bark and squared up, ready to be sawed into planks. Other timbers are still in the form of

Launching a Shipbuilding Career

For parents, apprenticeship was a good way to launch their son on the path to a good career. However, some apprentices were orphans or boys whose parents could not afford to keep them. Apprenticeship could last any number of years, depending on the boy's age. Francis Hattaway of Virginia was apprenticed to "learn the trade of a sawyer" (someone who saws wood) when he was only five years old.

When an apprentice's training was over, the master presented him with his "freedom dues," or what the master had promised in the contract to provide him upon completion of his service and training. Usually, this consisted of two suits of clothes—a rough suit for working and a finer suit for Sundays. Some masters even supplied a set of tools. After apprenticeship, the young man became a journeyman. Then he could work for any master and earn wages. Once he could afford it, he might even open his own shipyard. Many English journeymen came to the colonies for better work opportunities.

rough logs. Pine timbers are a special case. Their tall, straight trunks make the best wood for ships' masts. The pine timbers are soaking in a mast pond. This keeps the pine's pitch, or resin, from drying out so the mast will not crack.

Down toward the water's edge, ships' carpenters are inspecting their handiwork. Last week they began work on a new ship by laying the **keel**. This long, thick wooden beam is like the ship's spine. It runs along the bottom of the vessel from bow to stern, or front to back. (*Bow* rhymes with "how.") Now the keel rests on the stocks, the bed of squared timbers where the ship will stay until it is done. The carpenters have bolted a stem post on the front of the keel and a stern post on the rear. These two posts form an upward angle on the two ends of the ship.

Nearby, another ship is taking shape on its stocks. With the keel in place, the carpenters are now at work on the **hull**. This is the shell of the ship. It could be fat-bellied for large cargo ships, or it could be narrower and sleeker for fishing or coastal trading. The carpenters have already attached curved wooden ribs to the keel to make the frame, or skeleton of the ship. It outlines the ship's shape. Today they are beginning to fasten planking to the frame to form the outside of the hull.

Two workers in a sawmill in Colonial Williamsburg, Virginia.

The Daily Routine

The workday goes on, with teams of workers busy at their special tasks like bees in a hive. All the while, laborers cross the shipyard carrying timbers on their shoulders, and young boys with buckets or tools scurry about on errands. The ring of hammers and the rasp of the saws echo throughout the shipyard.

After a couple of hours' work, the shipbuilders are getting hungry. The foreman gives them half an hour off to eat breakfast, which might consist of bread or cold leftovers. Then it is back to work until 11:00 A.M., when the welcome call of "Grog-O!" rings out across the shipyard. At once, all the workers drop their tools and rush to the workhouse for a refreshing mug of grog. This is a weak mixture of water and rum, often with lemon or lime juice added. For workers who have been sweating all morning, the grog replaces their lost body fluids.

In the early afternoon, everyone gets an hour off for dinner. This is the midday meal that we call lunch. The grog ritual is repeated at 4:00 P.M., and work resumes again. Finally, around 7:15, it is time to go home.

After supper with their families, the shipbuilders will not stay up long. They are worn out from a hard day's work, and they do not want to waste the precious candles that light their homes. Morning will come soon and Sunday, the one day off, is still far away. Sinking into a straw-stuffed mattress, each weary worker collapses into bed.

Some of the tools a colonial shipbuilder used.

THREE

A Closer Look

As the owner looks out over his shipyard, he sees many groups of craftspeople at work on their special tasks. Each task is a part of the whole. The master shipbuilder began his career as a boy, and he has helped with many of these jobs himself. He knows how they should be done. Throughout the day, he makes the rounds of each work area to get a closer look.

The Sawyer

The sawyers work in pairs, sawing timbers with a long, two-handled saw. They position the wood over a long hole in the ground called a sawpit. Some shipyards covered their sawpit with a roof or built a sawhouse around it. Then the sawyers could still work when it was raining.

To saw a timber into planks, one sawyer stands up on top of the timber, and his partner stands down in the pit. The

Complex gear and rigging on tall ships of the Maine Windjammer Association.

top sawyer was usually the owner of the saw, and he kept it sharpened. Each sawyer holds one handle of the saw. The top sawyer pulls up, then the bottom sawyer pulls down. Over and over they saw, gradually moving down the length of the timber until they reach the end. Once they finish sawing a timber, they stack the wood nearby and begin on another timber.

Sawing was backbreaking labor. Sawyers sweated profusely, especially in the summer. The bottom sawyer had another disadvantage. Sawdust showered down on him all day long, getting into his eyes, nose, and mouth.

The Ship's Carpenter

The ship's carpenter fits the wood parts together and nails them into place. His hammer is a wooden mallet, and his nails are wooden pegs called treenails—pronounced "trunnels." First he uses an auger to drill holes where the pegs will go. Then, after pounding each peg in, he uses a narrow iron tool called a pin maul to drive the nail deeper than the wood's surface. This is called countersinking the nail.

Sawyers using a pit saw at Colonial Williamsburg, Virginia.

Many parts of the ship's hull are made of curved wood. For planking, the carpenter softens the planks with steam, putting them into a steam box for a while. He bends the planks into shape as he nails them to the hull. Then they follow the gentle curve that enables the ship to glide through the water.

The curved ribs of the ship's frame have to be strong and unbendable. As the ship's foundation, they carry great weight and endure heavy stress. For these, the carpenter often uses wood from trees that naturally grow in a curve. If the grain of the wood follows the curve, it is less likely to crack under pressure. No tree trunk would grow as curvy as a rib had to be, though. So the carpenter makes each rib by piecing together several curved pieces of wood called futtocks. For large ships, it took as many as a dozen or more futtocks to make one rib.

Knees are a special case. The knees are blocks of wood that join the hull to the deck. Knees are useful braces in many other parts of the ship's construction. They bend at a square angle, like a person's bent knee. For strength, a knee had to be one piece of wood that grew in a bent direction. Shipbuilders found this shape of wood at the point where a limb branches out from the trunk. Oak trees were the best species for knees. Their wood was very hard, their branches were thick, and their branching pattern was just right for a knee's angle.

Carpenters have been busy for weeks on the frame and planking of this ship. They also lay planks for the deck, the "top floor" of the ship, where people walk around. Meanwhile, the joiner goes about his own tasks.

The Joiner

The joiner is a carpenter who cuts and fits wood together with joints instead of nails. He uses many types of planes—wooden tools with an iron blade—for shaving, smoothing, and gouging wood. Then he drives the joints together using a wooden mallet.

One of the joiner's tasks is to install the rails that run around the top of the deck. For this he makes a mortise-and-tenon joint, fitting the end of one piece of wood into a hole in another piece. Another task is to finish off the captain's cabin. Here he builds a chest of drawers to hold the logbook, charts (maps), and other equipment. For this, the joiner fits the edges of the furniture together using dovetail joints. The corners interlock the way you might cross your fingers between each other.

The Caulker

Once the ship's planking is in place, the caulkers go to work. Caulkers seal every seam where water might seep into the ship. For this, they use **oakum**, or wads of tarred hemp fibers. Oakum was made simply by unraveling tarred rope. Children, with their small hands, were good workers for this task.

The caulker fills the cracks between planks of wood on the hull and deck. He seals every joint the joiner has made and even fills in oakum around every treenail. First the caulker stuffs oakum into the space. Then he tamps it in tightly, using a flat tool called a caulking iron that he pounds with his mallet.

Just a few more steps are left before the ship can be launched. Soon the smell of tar fills the air as workers bring out steamy barrels of the sticky black stuff. They paint the underside of the hull with tar to seal it. The tar keeps water from seeping in and rotting the hull. It also keeps out the dreaded shipworms that bore holes into the wood.

At last the ship's hull is complete. Adding the masts and sails is the last step in finishing the ship. However, those tasks are usually not done on land. Now is the time to launch the hull into the water. Although the shipbuilders are sure of their skills, one question lurks in the back of everyone's mind: Will it float?

FOUR

The Shipbuilder's Community

The master shipbuilder studies his tide charts to figure out the best time for the launch. Tides are the twice-daily rise and fall of the water level, and ships are always launched during high tide. With water reaching high on the shore, the ship is less likely to scrape the bottom once it enters the water.

On the day set for the launch, shipyard workers snap into action. They lay out more timbers, making a pathway from the stocks down to the water's edge. The ship will slide along the timbers and splash right into the water. Meanwhile, news of the launch has spread around town. A launch is such an important event that many of the townspeople show up to watch. Schools even close so the children can come and watch.

At last the moment arrives. All the work teams in the shipyard drop their tools and rush to the launch site. Some help, while others just gaze with pride at the object of their labor. Heaving and straining, workers pull on ropes to drag the ship along the timbers. Into the water it glides—and it floats! At once a great cheer rises up from the crowd.

A Community Project

It is no wonder that so many townspeople turned out for the launch. Shipbuilding was a community project in many ways. Almost everyone in a shipyard town had a family member or friend who helped build the ships. Nearly every type of craftsperson in town played a part. Until

Unfurling a sail on the rebuilt colonial ship Godspeed.

the mid-1700s, most shipwrights imported ropes, sails, and other gear from England. Gradually, though, people in colonial seaports developed their own crafts to support shipbuilding.

In 1749, a Boston resident wrote that shipbuilding is "one of the greatest Articles of our Trade and Manufacture." The shipbuilding business, he said, "[employs] and maintains above 30 Denominations of Tradesmen and Artificers." Those tradesmen included rope makers, sail makers, blacksmiths, and

Dashing the Bottle

For Laurence Bradford of Duxbury, Massachusetts, the launching of a ship was a highlight of his childhood days. He recalled, "The most interesting part of the programme to us small boys was what we called 'dashing the bottle.'" A man stood out on the bow holding a rope tied to a bottle of wine. Just as the ship slipped into the water, he dashed the bottle against the bow, shouting, "Here's success to the good ship *Nathaniel!*"—or whatever the ship's name was. The tradition of "dashing the bottle" is still followed when ships are launched today, usually with champagne and typically carried out by a woman.

many others. Their handcrafted goods were added to the ship after it was launched.

The Rope Maker

One important step in finishing a ship was to install all the ropes needed to hold things in place and adjust the sails. Ropes were also known as cordage, and the entire setup of ropes and sails was the ship's rigging. Every shipbuilding city had at least one ropewalk, a factory where cordage was made. People had to walk a long way to get from one end of the ropewalk to the other. Ropewalks were strung out for hundreds of feet to make room for long strands of rope.

John Daniel, Boston's largest rope maker in the 1740s, managed a ropewalk that was 780 feet long—more than one-seventh of a mile. Nearby were smaller sheds for making yarn. Daniel made every type of cordage, from yarn and twine to heavy ropes many inches thick. Ships' rope was in such demand that, by 1794, Boston had fourteen ropewalks.

Inside the ropewalk, both people and machines worked with fibers of the hemp plant. These fibers were easy to bend and twist, yet they were very strong. First the fibers were combed and straightened. Next they were spun into yarn, often with child workers turning the giant spinning wheels. Laurence Bradford worked at a Massachusetts ropewalk as a child. "It was monotonous work, the spinning," he recalled, "and the boy turning the wheel that twisted the threads had a dull time of it; . . . he heard nothing but the rattle of his wheel. . . ." Rope was such a high-demand product that it led to widespread hemp farming throughout the colonies. In Pennsylvania, a leading agricultural producer, hemp was second only to wheat.

Shipbuilders need two types of rope. Tarred rope was used

The maze of rigging on a colonial sailing ship.

for standing rigging, or rope that stayed in place. It was tied to masts, for example, to hold them in place. Yarn for tarred rope was soaked in steaming kettles of tar to make it waterproof and keep it from rotting. "White rope" was used for running rigging, or ropes that sailors pulled to move sails and spars. Tar stiffened a rope, but white rope had to bend, slip, and slide smoothly through hands and metal rings. After spinning, the yarn was twisted on a machine into strands as long as the ropewalk. Finally, several strands were twisted together to make a rope. Ropewalks provided plenty of work for unskilled day laborers—men, women, and children—in port cities up and down the coast.

The Sail Maker

A sail maker's workshop had to be spacious enough to spread out a large sail on the floor. These shops were often located on the upper story of a warehouse. Up there in the loft, no supporting beams rose up from the floor. Thus the sail maker's shop was called a sail loft.

To make a sail, the master sail maker first purchased sailcloth from a local textile mill or bought it from merchants who imported it from English mills. Then he outlined a sail's size and shape on the floor of the sail loft with twine. He secured the corners of the outline with an awl, a sharp tool for punching holes. Next he laid out sailcloth underneath the twine pattern. Sailcloth, or canvas, was woven out of hemp or linen fibers. Then he cut the cloth around the pattern, leaving a few inches around the edges for a hem.

A Citywide Industry

Building just one ship could boost the economy of an entire city. As an example, John Banister was a merchant in Newport, Rhode Island. In 1740, he ordered the construction of the *Leathley*, a 300-ton merchant ship. Banister's accounts show that it took twenty-three different crafts to build his ship. The list included shipwrights, joiners, carvers, cabinetmakers, block makers, small-boat builders, rope makers, riggers, sail makers, blacksmiths, painters, and bricklayers. Banister paid for founders to cast iron, braziers to make brass, glaziers to make glass, and coopers to make barrels. His vessel required the services of ten ship chandlers, or dealers who sell ships' supplies. They provided nails, bolts, hinges, anchors, and other goods. Carpenters worked from dawn to dusk, and Newport's butchers and bakers kept everyone fed. Hardly anyone in town was untouched by Banister's shipbuilding project.

Completely flat sails would not "belly out" to catch the wind. A master sail maker knew how to make a sail that would swell in a slight balloon shape. For one thing, he cut the foot, or bottom of the sail, in a slight curve. More important, he did not make the sail out of just one piece of cloth. Instead, he laid out several wide panels of sailcloth side by side, with their edges overlapping to allow for seams. When he stitched the seams, he varied their width so the sail did not lay flat but had a fat bulge.

Like all master craftspeople, the sail maker had apprentices and other helpers. They sewed rope around the edges of the sail, using a wide, dull-pointed needle and twine. They forced the needle through the thick canvas with the palm, a leather strap worn around the hand. Along the top of the sail, they attached grommets, or donut-shaped metal rings. Ropes would run through the grommets to hold the sail onto the spar. Ropes along the foot were extended to make the clews, or lower corners, of the sail. Clews needed special treatment. They were pulled, stretched, and tugged throughout a voyage to adjust the sails. They had to stand up to a lot of stress. Workers wound yarn, tarred cloth, and twine around the clew. Finally, they bent it into a loop that ropes could run through.

Sail makers stitching canvas in a sail loft in Maine.

Other Craftspeople

Many other craftspeople contributed their skills to completing the
ship. A blacksmith heated and hammered iron to make the ship's
anchor. Boat builders made small rowboats to mount on the side of
the ship. They were used mainly on fishing vessels to move quickly
into schools of fish, cast nets, and harpoon and tow whales. The
boats were also used for rowing to shore or as lifeboats in case of
emergency. Block makers crafted devices containing pulleys, or
grooved wheels, for ropes to run through. A rope was tied to an

object and strung through the block, while someone pulled the other end of the rope. This way, a sailor could smoothly lift sails, cargo, and other heavy items.

Finishing the Ship

Now that the ship is afloat, workers move it close to the shore. Their next task is to step the mast, or set it in place. First they tie several ropes to the mast. Then, sweating and groaning, they strain on the ropes to hoist the mast into an upright position. Next they lower it down through a hole in the deck until it drops into a hollowed-out space in the keel called the step. That is why this job is called stepping the mast. Following a long tradition, a coin has been placed into the hollow, where it will rest at the bottom of the mast. The coin is a good-luck token for a safe voyage. Up above deck, ropes are tied to the mast to hold it firmly in place.

Skilled workers attach the spars and mount the sails, fitting and stretching them into place. They rig the ropes, running them through blocks, sails, and spars in an elaborate web. Rowboats are attached to the sides of the ship. At last it is ready for its voyage. If all goes well, the ship will spend many years upon the sea. It is a beautiful work of art, the pride of colonial craftsmanship, and the work of many hands.

The Figurehead

Shipbuilders often mounted a figurehead on the bow of the ship. Figureheads were decorative wooden sculptures of people, animals, or other figures. For people, a figurehead depicted the entire body, the upper half of the body, or just the head and shoulders. Popular male figures were modeled after the ship owner, a famous leader, or an American Indian. Female figures featured a Greek or Roman goddess or the ship owner's wife or daughter. For animals, the American eagle was a favorite. The figurehead might show an eagle with its wings spread or just the eagle's head. Other animals might be a lion or a deer. Some shipbuilders simply used a decorative curly design. This tradition of adding a figurehead to a ship comes from ancient times, when sailors believed the figurehead's eyes would see the ship safely through its voyage.

FIVE

New Ships for a New Nation

Tensions between the colonies and their mother country grew over time as Britain imposed more trade rules and taxes on the colonists. Merchants saw the new rules and taxes as a violation of their liberty. Shipbuilders worried that these measures would reduce trade and the demand for ship production. Eventually, the colonists fought the Revolutionary War (1775–1783) to gain their independence. Then they could control their own trade, too. Many ships that the colonists had built took part in the war. After their victory, the colonies became the United States of America. The new nation was fortunate to have developed its shipbuilding industry so well. It now had its own fleet of merchant ships. By 1797, the United States had its own naval warships—the USS *Constitution* and the USS *Constellation*.

Scene at sunset in Boston Harbor in the days of the great sailing ships.

After the war, shipbuilding expanded tremendously. No longer were the former colonies hampered by British rules and regulations. Great shipyards flourished all along the coast, from Maine and Massachusetts in the north to South Carolina and Georgia in the south. They sent thousands of well-built ships out to sea.

Steam and Iron

Many aspects of the shipbuilding craft changed in the years to come. For centuries, ships were powered by wind filling their sails. In the 1700s, engineers began trying to build steam-powered ship. They burned coal or wood to boil water and produce steam. The steam power then turned paddle wheels or propellers that moved the ship through the water. Robert Fulton launched his first paddle-wheeled steamboat in the early 1800s. By the 1850s, the U.S. Navy was adding steamships to its fleet. Most early steamships used a combination of sails and steam power.

In the mid-1800s, battleship designers began experimenting with ironclad ships. At first, ironclads had wooden frames

Robert Fulton's 1807 Clermont *paddle-wheeled steamboat could reach a speed of 5 miles per hour.*

covered with iron or steel plates. As time went on, more and more wooden parts were replaced with iron. The first battle between ironclad warships took place during the U.S. Civil War (1861–1865). The *Monitor* and the *Merrimack* were the players in this famous naval battle of 1862. Historians still argue about which ship won. Still, the battle taught navies around the world how tough ironclads could be.

The Craft Lives On

Iron and steam changed the shipbuilding craft but did not destroy it. Many traditional shipyards did go out of business. Others converted their operations to make the new vessels. In spite of new developments, many aspects of shipbuilding stayed the same. The basic designs of the hull and the structures that keep it afloat have not changed over time.

Meanwhile, some shipbuilders held on to the art of building wooden sailing ships. The mid-1900s saw a new interest in "tall ships"—large vessels with traditional sails billowing from their tall masts. At the same time, shipbuilders here and there along the coast revived the colonial shipbuilding craft. One example is a project at Historic Jamestowne. This is the site where settlers established the Virginia colony in 1607. They arrived in three

The USS Constitution, *the world's oldest commissioned warship, afloat in Boston Harbor.*

ships—the *Susan Constant*, the *Godspeed*, and the *Discovery*.

To honor the settlement's 350th anniversary, shipbuilders built replicas of these three ships in 1957. More recently, shipbuilders and historians fashioned newer and more accurate re-creations, using the same methods and skills of colonial times, for the 400th anniversary in 2007. Visitors can climb aboard the ships and marvel at the centuries-old craft of shipbuilding. Running a hand along the shiny planks or the maze of twisted ropes, they imagine the shipbuilders who spent their lives at the craft.

Glossary

apprentices	young people who train under a master craftsperson to learn a trade
cargo	a load of goods carried by land, sea, or air
colonial	relating to colonies
colonists	people who settle a new land for their home country
cove	a coastal bay or inlet
hull	the main body of a ship
indentured servants	people who provide their labor to pay for their trip to a new land
journeyman	a craftsperson who has completed an apprenticeship and may work for wages
keel	the "spine" of a ship, stretching along the center of the ship's bottom
merchants	businesspeople who sell goods to others
oakum	hemp fibers soaked in tar and used to seal the gaps between a ship's planks
planks	long, flat wooden boards
shipwrights	another name for shipbuilders
shipyard	large work area where shipbuilding takes place
spars	wooden poles at the top and bottom of sails
timber	live trees in a forest; also, cut-down tree trunks that are ready to be sawed
tonnage	the size of a ship, measured in terms of how much cargo it can carry

Find Out More

BOOKS

Bailey, Gerry. *Sea Transportation: Discover Science Through Facts and Fun.* Pleasantville, NY: Gareth Stevens, 2009.

Kalman, Bobby. *A Visual Dictionary of a Colonial Community.* New York: Crabtree Publishing, 2008.

Roberts, Russell. *Life in Colonial America.* Hockessin, DE: Mitchell Lane Publishers, 2008.

Winters, Kay, and Larry Day (illustrator). *Colonial Voices: Hear Them Speak.* New York: Dutton Children's Books, 2008.

WEBSITES

Colonial Kids: A Celebration of Life in the 1700s
http://library.thinkquest.org/J002611F/
Find out what colonial children wore, what their communities were like, and how they worked and played.

Liberty's Kids: Now and Then
http://www.libertyskids.com/nowthen/index.html
Here you will learn about life in the 1700s and how it compares with life today.

Massachusetts Maritime Museums
http://www.maritimemuseums.net/MA.html
This site lists more than three dozen Massachusetts museums and historic sites related to ships and shipbuilding.
Note: Many other coastal states have their own maritime museums.

Replica of Jamestown Ship Built in Maine
http://www.history.com/videos/replica-of-jamestown-ship-built-in-maine#replica-of-jamestown-ship-built-in-maine
Watch videos of shipbuilders constructing a replica of the 1607 colonial ship *Godspeed.*

Index

Page numbers in **boldface** are illustrations.

About the Author

Ann Heinrichs is the author of more than 200 books for children and young adults. Most of them cover U.S. and world history, geography, culture, and political affairs. Ann was a children's book editor for many years. Then she worked as an advertising copywriter. An avid traveler, she has toured Europe, Asia, Africa, and the Middle East. Born in Fort Smith, Arkansas, she now lives in Chicago, Illinois. She enjoys bicycling and kayaking.